# About the Pc_.

Possibly better known poetically these days for his syndicated radio show Beyond Poetry, which he shares with stations around the world, Dean Fraser previously spent years touring extensively. Learning his craft in front of live audiences and understanding just what makes an effective poem work. This book marks his fifth poetry collection to date and as well as his books, he has been published in many international magazines including New Dawn, Kindred Spirit and Fate & Fortune, to mention only a few. Far from being solely a poet, Dean Fraser writes well-being and self-realization books, giving talks on how slight changes in our mindset can help us all to live a more harmonious life. He became known as The Quantum Poet when a radio presenter many years ago referred to him that way throughout an hour-long interview (he never did find out why!) Dean did like the name though and kept it.

www.facebook.com/thequantumpoet

80 525 30 X

# Other Titles by Dean Fraser

## Poetry

### Non-Poetry

# Beyond Poetry

_All the best_

_Dean fra_

## Celebrating Nature and Life

Dean Fraser

The Quantum Poet

ISBN 9781548066659

www.facebook.com/thequantumpoet

# Beyond
# Poetry

# Contents

# Introduction

Welcome to my first brand new poetry collection for over two years!

Writing these poems has been a thoroughly enjoyable experience, for the first time in my poetic career I truly took my time in the crafting of the tales I wanted to tell. For once there were no deadlines to meet or an upcoming tour the book had to be completed for. Inspiration came from many sources ranging from ancient legends and folklore through to contemporary life in the 21st Century.

My decision right from the beginning was to create a collection of exquisitely beautiful poems. I wanted these poetic tales to stand the test of time, to be as relevant and appreciated in a hundred years, as I aimed for them to be today.

I called this book Beyond Poetry, with a wish for this collection to be my gift to you, my readers.

Poetic echoes.

Dean Fraser – The Quantum Poet

# A True Community

Farming
Growing
Fertile land
Feeding so many

A bus passes through
But only on a Thursday
Eleven on the dot it leaves
To return at three
A chance to visit the metropolis
The big town
Some forty thousand people all told
Sensory overload
Here exist less human souls
Many less
A thousand
Maybe

Village life
Provisions store
It's privately owned
Chain store free zone
Two years ago the post office closed
And with it a century old way of life

A hairdresser
I'm not acquainted with
A beauty therapist
I'm reasonably well acquainted with
The library visits us
On wheels
Twice a month
Literary lifeline

Carl runs the garage
Failing to understand any car made after '95
Suits most of us well
Perfection
Two churches
Take your pick
According to faith

Living by the seasons
Harmony with nature
Working alongside her
A village green
For all the world
Like a thousand jigsaw images

Three pubs await our custom
Each has a darts team
Speaking volumes about our main pastime

Has the English village changed?

Maybe
Well, okay
Yes
Some things remain
Characters
All life going on
Community
Sure, everyone knows your business
May it forever remain
A true community

*I have experienced life in several English villages and may they exist forever…evolving, yet remaining constant*

# A Tale of Two Trains

Up to one hundred and twenty-five miles an hour they say
Free wi-fi, charge your phone as you travel on your way
Streamlined Pendolino trains miracle of this hi-tech existence
Kick back, have a coffee, you won't feel the distance
Doors open, another town before us can wait no more
In my mind I travel back, right back to glorious days of yore

Up to one hundred and twenty-six miles an hour records say
At the helm driver Joe Duddington alongside fireman Bray
Streamlined Mallard to Sir Nigel Gresley owed its existence
Faster and faster she went over the measured distance
The record still holds, and probably will for ever more
She survives, archaic reminder of those glorious days of yore

*It seems nothing is new, wonderful though modern Pendolino trains are, in 1938 steam could match it for speed (if not eco-friendliness)*

# The Jacket

Her most treasured possession
Fraying
Veritably threadbare
Once brown
Now no longer
Original colour faded out
Existing only in memory
As he does now
Grandpops
Her adored Grandpops

Three years since he passed away
His jacket
The one he wore come rain or shine
Became hers
Only hers
And the emotions
Which came with it
She wore it every day
His jacket
Come rain or shine
He somehow feeling closer
Protecting her even now
As he once had

What now?
As the jacket
His jacket
Borrowed from him
On permanent loan
Now worn by her
Gently wears out
She cries
Tears of despair
What now?
No amount of cleaning
Of repairing
Patching up
Can save it
Things wear out
Memories don't
What now?

A suggestion arrives from afar
Grandpops lives in you
In those treasured times
His words of love
Of humour
His jacket
Your jacket
The symbol
Of all he was
Find an exact replica
Have one made if needs be

Like when it was new
When Grandpops wore it the first time
It's the remembrance
Deep inside
Your new jacket
Worn
In honour of his jacket
It will still hold the memories
Every single one of them

New jacket
Same old warmth

So she did
And it does
Comforts her
This new jacket
Exactly like before
Worn with love

What of Grandpops old jacket?
Framed, it hangs in her den
She smiles up at it
And dances a happy dance
Just as she did with Grandpops
So many times
Wearing her
His jacket

# Nature Freely Gives

Jack In The Green awakens from his slumber
Spring is upon us, nature in all her wonder
Gaze in awe of rebirth, renewal, fertility
Stood deep in the forest, deep within tranquillity

Robin Goodfellow his mischief to perform
Souring milk, trampling crop circles from fields of corn
Tripping those who into the green wood unwary tread
Laughing, yet another traveller away from path he led

Puck so much more than a Midsummer Night's Dream
Shakespeare drawing upon history, the arcane, unseen
Trickster of faery folk, denizen of mischievous games and fun
Beware, if he enchants you, from those woods you'll never run

Herne the Hunter now be wary here, take heed
Horns upon his head, the wildest wild hunt he leads
Terrified peasants flee from upon his path
Lest they feel the full forth of his awful wrath

Robin Hood, legend tells many tales of his noble deeds
Taking only from rich, to the poor sharing his proceeds
Did he exist, the debate lingers on, I think live he once must
With his merry band, close to nature, righting the unjust

The Green Man, guardian of all that truly matters
Without the woods, forest, trees, our ecosystem shatters
Summer sun to winter's frozen whitest beauty
He oversees it all, such is The Green Man's duty

Of all these characters who's stories I shared this day
A common thread exists and I feel compelled to say
Treasure the green wood, as all nature freely gives
Knowing any less than that is to hardly even live

*These faery folk, Robin Hood and The Green Man have come down to us from ancient ballad and poetry writers, that these stories have survived down through millennia only serves to underline their continued relevance and importance to us in this time*

# Be Beautiful...

It's all around if we open our eyes to see
Today I saw a gorgeous tree
Growing out of an old crumbling wall
There lies beauty
It's everywhere around
And it costs nothing

*I am giving beauty the chance it deserves*

# I'm What's His Face

The presenting of many a poetic radio show
Doesn't ensure recognition wherever I go
Live performances to varied venues I travel
An hour or two of attention as poetic tales unravel
Television interviews thrust me into the spotlight
Talking of poems and the other words I write
Why The Quantum Poet invariably they ask
TV friendly sound-bites becoming my main task
Next happens probingly enquiring of my aspirations
Shortly followed by wishing to know my inspirations
I say hip hop and rap are poetry, they usually agree
How long have I been writing and what next for me?
A legacy for future generations I assert is crucial
And telling how to buy my books especially useful
So passes by another fifteen or thirty minutes of fame
Don't get me wrong I love appearing on TV all the same
Especially when the supermarket queue I later grace
As an inquisitive soul asks "Aren't you what's his face?"

*What it is like being recognised and yet apparently not quite able to be placed, although I have happily had people come up to me in a mall to recite their poetry and it is lovely, I always give them some of my attention and time*

# The Drawer in the Mine

He a drawer deep underground
A driver of ponies
Of small stature
Perfectly suited to task
His job
Other men toiling
Inching forward each day
Filling tubs with black gold
Coal to fuel
Keeping the wheels of industry turning
The drawer, Robert Hampson his name
Subterranean friend to pit ponies
Moving impossibly heavy loads
Making way for yet more back-breaking work
And yet it was his destiny
All he knew
He didn't have to dig like so many
His father and grandfather before him
They had been drawers
Knowing horses right there in his blood
His genes
Soon he would leave the mine
New experiences

Life always changes
The unexpected happens
Yet for his time
Deep in the mine
He was happy

*A drawer used to be responsible for transporting coal from the face to the surface. This is part of the story of my own great grandfather, for more of his tale and to see where he went next, have a look at the poem Boots 2 in my book The Lancashire Poems*

# Have a Good Day, Mr Magpie

La Gazza Ladra, Rossini gave us an opera
The Thieving Magpie his choice of drama
Cunning avian immortalized by nursery rhyme
One for what was it? The magpie's next crime?
This Al Capone of flight, gangster bird, larger than life
Intelligence is here, quick thinking, sharper than a knife
Other birds shun it, does it feel or even care?
All I know when spotted by me unless in a pair
A solitary magpie always evokes the same response
A salute from me and quickly muttered once
"Hello Mr Magpie, how's your wife and kids?"
Any other words superstition strictly forbids
The curse now suitably broken yet again
Dignity I can attempt to somehow regain

*I have wanted to write of magpies for a while and yes, I really do go through all that performance when I spot a solitary one*

# The Old Straight Track

The greenest valley spread far and wide
Slowly settlement starts on either side
Bronze age people, eventually two villages grew
Looking from a distance at one another, what next to do?
Great plans are conceived, as elders confer to discuss
To be better able to trade, a track we'll make between us
The Dodman by description, early surveyor of the land
Making sure the track was straight by his own fair hand
And straight for sure it became, shortest route attainable
Two villages connected in peace, with a bond unbreakable
Trading, marrying with their neighbours in the valley
A thousand years or more co-existing quite happily

An invasion, alien ways, ruled by another hand
Roman legions taking over exactly as planned
The people settled eventually, amicable existence
Alongside the Romans, yet still kept their distance
Across the valley, the villas and bathhouses grew
Centurions marched the old straight track anew
The gromatici, Roman surveyor, got a commendation
Made the track their own through their time of occupation

Middle ages two villages either side of the valley floor

People travelled on horse, just as on foot once before
Taken for granted, the old track, as history unfolded
The industrial revolution next upon the scene exploded
A great engineer had a plan, Brunel by name
Unite this land together and do it by train
Our valley he viewed, surveyed and found it good
We'll lay track here, using the old route we should
Two villages either side of the valley, connected by steam
Twenty minutes' journey must have seemed like a dream
A hundred years the villages prospered, became rich
Track surviving two wars, trains continued without a hitch

1960's the railways needed to profit, pay their way
Dr Beeching tasked to make it happen, the final say
Brutally, with logic his tool, he closed stations and lines
To the old straight track the end, it seems had come the time
Two villages either side of the valley far and wide
No longer connected, their togetherness just died
Three thousand years of harmony gone in a flash
Community sacrificed over the gods of hard cash
The old route overgrown, for the first time unused
What now, to disappear forever, train track removed

Twenty first century begins, looking forward at the past
A local Council meeting and a question finally asked
"let's make a footpath, across the valley floor
Connect the two villages once again, like before"
It came to pass, the way cleared, gravel lain
A new era, new time, the old track born again

Along the way picking up a national tourism award
Ten years it's been open, it's future now assured
Two villages, countless generations been and gone
Yet all have enjoyed the old straight track to walk upon

# Never Meet Your Heroes

Melting clocks
The memory persists
A moment of genius
Pure sublime
Symbolism
And yet so much more
Inspired so many childish artistic endeavours
My tentative ventures into art
Paint
Immortalized in my paint
Still the memory persists
Drawing me in
To see
Needing to see
Reach out into the painting
What was the artist feeling?
Could I feel it too?
Compelled to witness first hand
And I did
Tiny in proportion
This giant of influence
In the gallery
Having it to myself

Quiet time of the day
Stood
Studying
Stunned
And I felt
Well
Less impressed now
Oddly considerably less impressed

*In 2006 I travelled to The Museum of Modern Art in New York to fulfil a childhood dream to see Dali's The Persistence of Memory and found myself slightly underwhelmed, although I did love discovering Van Gogh - he hadn't been lost, I just never really noticed his work before!*

# The Dancers of Life

Sticks clash together as the bells ring
Heralding Centuries old rites of spring
Morris Men dancing in each season
Each well-rehearsed step for a reason
The fiddle player keeping with tradition
Lending the dance for all his rhythm
Denizen of all things beauteous and green
The village has chosen The May Queen
Morris Men dancing good harvest to bring
Then the fool is crowned the misrule King
The green wood, the field ripe with corn
From winter's deathly hold, spring is reborn
Every jig performed, every "hey" and every dance
If you be lucky enough to watch them perchance
Be sure to applaud and treat them with respect
They do this for all of us, mother nature to protect

In market square or village green the dance goes on
Through countless generations and the dance goes on
Right across this fairest land forever the dance goes on

*The first written record of Morris Men dates back six centuries and
the tradition was already ancient even then*

# The Shaman in the Park

He walks as he chants, feeling the grass beneath his feet
Smiling inwardly, he knows who he came here to meet
Sacred sounds reverberate, into air and within the ground
Soon it happens, by him they swoop, begin to fly around
Warmer weather is here, swallows confirming this
As by fractions of a centimetre our shaman they miss
Feeling his energy, chanting he continues, projecting love
Dancing aerially around him, they skim his arms held above
Then the spell is broken, a curious dog barks its presence
Birds flee, the shaman gives thanks and returns to the present

*A story of your poet and his communication with nature, in this case perhaps twenty or so swallows recently returned to these shores to enjoy the summer warmth*

# Linger a Little Longer

Linger a little longer in our home
Before once again you must roam
Tell us of your travellers' tales
Spare us none of the details

Stay with us, more precious stories
Of strangest lands and territories
Those desert sunsets you bore witness
Your need to go when you feel listless

Yet talk some more and lay down here
Of more adventures we long to hear
The silk route taken and the olive trail
Of every mountain you had to scale

Be with us for a little more time
Share our food, drink our wine
Regale us with happy song and dance
Full of mystery and a little romance

Rest awhile our dearest friend
We know to journeys you must attend

Linger a little longer with us right here
For all too soon you will disappear

*The story of an adventurous friend who is absolutely compelled to travel, new horizons constantly call her*

# Connected Through Time and Sword

PART ONE

No more the battlefield for him
No more kill or be killed
A life he had known since he cared to remember
Cast aside
As he now casts aside the tools of death

He makes his way
Avenue of standing stones he knows so well
Island in the lake his destination
Sacred place of ritual
Across timber walkway he crosses

His brother had died by the sword
Fallen in battle like so many
He felt world weary
Once his father had fallen also
He felt oh so world weary

His finest bronze sword in his hand
Like so many times before
This time the reason differed

This time he came in peace
To make peace

Raising his sword high above his head
His shout heard all across the valley
"Goddess take my sword
in peace I choose to live!"
Casting it into the lake

He watched for a while
Ripples settling on the water
Then calmness, as he now felt inside
Taking his leave of that place
And his former life

PART TWO

He sought to understand
This man of learning
Professorship was one thing
Hands-on his eternal passion
Archaeology means digging

This site drew him
Like moth to flame
Coursing deep through his blood
Feeling kinship to this place
To know more

Our ancestors, his ancestors
Ancient landscape he could read
The lake still seen in his mind's eye
Now long silted up
Mound signified the island

Experience told him Bronze Age
He felt sure
Excavation
Reaching into the past
A glimpse into lives long gone

And then they found it
Dirt encrusted it saw daylight once again
Even after all these years
All those digs
He felt the familiar thrill

Later, cleaned and preserved
This legacy from another time
Was it ritual?
Cast into the water as sacrifice?
He sat in quiet contemplation

Then suddenly it overwhelmed him
Compelled to hold the sword
Feeling deep into the past
Through this sword...his ancestor spoke
And he saw and he understood

# Bodging in the Woods

A crafting bodger by trade is he
Residing in the woods he be
By the seasons he lives
Using what nature gives
Feeling every tree in the wood
Bodging runs deep in his blood
Spindles for chairs he makes
Only what he needs he takes
Coppicing his forest friends
The circles of life never ends
Spending his days productively
Furniture he crafts lovingly
Beauty in every knot, every joint
No nails or screws is the point
For here we have true art
Words alone cannot impart
Watch the bodger creating
His man powered lathe rotating
By chisel and saw, truly hand made
For his labours he is duly well paid
Yet for him the money matters not
It's about living here, in this spot
In touch with the past, nary a machine

At one with the woods and all that is green

*Bodgers are traditional craftsmen and women who live in the woods, expertly taking care of it and using only what they need to make their beautifully rustic wooden items. They go back far into antiquity. Here in England there are still a handful of people carrying on the trade, their creations are highly sought after and prized*

# Finding Himself in Nature

Deep in the heart of the forest
He lingers a moment to rest
He knows well his destination
Two hours meander his estimation
Finding the oldest tree of all, he hesitates
Sat, leant against the trunk he meditates

High within the mountain peaks
Within himself answers he seeks
All the world below somewhere
Quietly he finds his spot up there
Sheltered by cairn, thoughts he elevates
Gale rages all around as he meditates

Waves roar as they crash upon beach
Yet he's here some wisdom to reach
Upon his rock facing the wildest sea
Spray washed, alive he feels such empathy
As once again he enters altered states
In the heart of the storm, he meditates

Natural wonder he found all around
Emanating from deep within the ground

Carried on the wind, the rain and snow
Seeking answers in caves or plateau
Whatever journey he undertakes
Wherever he goes, he meditates

*I have meditated since my teenage years (a little while ago) and*
*although I love to meditate on trains, my preferred location is always*
*within nature*

# Fogou

Subterranean enigma the enduring mystery
Historians the use for which no two can agree
For storing grain, defences from attack or weather
Intuition speaks of a different role altogether

The wise man or woman, shaman of the clan
Their incantations and spells right there began
Entering the darkness of the fogou
These iron age magicians all knew
Deep within the womb of mother earth
Rituals of plentiful harvest were given birth
Fertility of the land ensured by their wisdoms
Protecting the people, chiefs and their kingdoms
Strange incantations long lost to the modern ear
Yet spend time in the fogou you might just hear
Words from aeons past travelling through time
A warning for us to take heed of their sign
To cherish this planet, feel how she lives
Taking from her only that she freely gives

*A fogou (pronounced foo-goo) is man-made subterranean iron-age
cave systems most famously found in Cornwall, England, yet also seen
in other places. Their precise use remains a mystery, ancient grain
particles were found in archaeological digs, leading some to think they*

*were for storage, my theory is these were offerings made to ensure a*
*good harvest*

# Acting Upon a Dream

A vision of another time
Feeling the landscape
Reaching into the past
Mineral rich
Quarry his location
Seeking
Seeking to communicate
Follow his intuition
Off the well walked track
Reading the ground
With closed eyes, he sees
And walks with purpose
Yes, it is just as he saw
Yes!

Hidden under long grass
This hollowed out depression
He drops to the ground
Hands feeling, seeing
As he knew it would be
This ancient smelting place
Suddenly his fingers touch something
Partly buried

Prising his prize from the Earth
Copper ore
Pure copper ore
What he came here for
Long thought long gone
He had a dream
Acted upon

This piece of rock
His gift
It is well travelled
Two continents it has visited
Held in such esteem
Treasured
It goes with him
Protective talisman
Or perhaps taliswoman
Copper of the goddess
She watches over him

*I travelled to a long disused quarry, after I saw it in a dream and found the small piece of pure copper ore mentioned in this poem. It has remained my constant companion for nearly two decades*

# Turner Surprise

Our pilgrimage in honour of his art
To nourish the soul, culture impart
Locations as our schedule can accommodate
Mentally travelling back in time to appreciate
Centuries on would he recognise the views?
Were he to stand here now, wearing our shoes
Genius of a bygone age, his legacy lives right on
A prize named after him, this artistic paragon
Wandering and wondering continued our quest
Finally overlooking the river, we linger to rest
And it happens, we look at one another, happy tears we cry
Laid out before us, the view he saw, and above a Turner sky

*A tribute to the painter J.M.W Turner, famous for his incredible skies
and the view he frequently painted of The River Thames from
Richmond Hill*

# The River and The Sea

A canoe launches into shallowest water
All but a stream
High in the mountains
Forward motion begins
Avoiding rocks
Patiently progress is made
Slowly yet surely
Widening and then
In an instant transformed
A cacophony of noise fills his ears
Rapids!
With long-won skill, he traverses
Shooting onwards
Summersaulting
Yet in control
Then calm returns
First signs of civilization
Ducks loudly announce their surprise
This alien intruder into their world
People fish along the banks
He steers a course away from their lines
Some wave hello
Others glare as his wake disturbs the fish

The town is reached
Graffiti he passes
Some is art made loud
Others proclaim allegiance to sports teams
Or unknown gangs
Two worlds co-exist here
Busy road and once busy river
Parallel
All activity going on
The people seemingly on fast-forward
Few spare him attention
As he breathes traffic pollution
Road left behind as a troubled memory
Into the park
Children wave
Raised paddle in salute
Smiling faces
Running along the banks
Then he's gone
Park also left behind
Other vessels use this river now
Pleasure boats, luxurious yachts
Gracing the harbour
His canoe tiny amongst the hustle and bustle
Four hours his journey
Travelling with the river
Today she co-operated
Let him pass in peace
He feels even tinier now

As into the sea he paddles
And he never felt so alive
He follows the coastline
Secluded bay
Far from people
Towering cliffs behind him
Canoe dragged upon the beach
Laying in the mid-day sun
Eating at last
Exhausted
Yet at peace

*An adventure following the call of the river from the mountains all the way to harbour and then sea*

# Tales to Tell

Fine jester in the court of noble king
Telling his stories in songs to sing
If he didn't please, he'd lose his head
Which would leave him feeling pretty dead

Music hall orator his tales shared
Before his audience his soul he bared
Needing to be fit, fast on his legs
If unliked he'd be pelted with eggs

Before them stood the poet tall
In tradition of jester and music hall
Hoping his audience wowed and awed
Then at the end they might just applaud

*My life as a twenty first century poetic story-teller is rather less*
*fraught with the dangers some of my predecessors had to endure*

# Mandolino

Smiling people gather round
Drawn by the beautiful sound
Across all of Europe and Africa
Italy, England across to Croatia
Keeping a tradition of millennia past
Reaching hearts in a way unsurpassed
Folk tunes or jazz it doesn't matter which
Such is the power it possesses to bewitch
As the music unfolds touching all deep within
The playing of a master of the mandolin

*Versions of a mandolin-like instrument have been played for over a thousand years, this poem is dedicated to the brilliant Chris Leslie, multi-instrumentalist and a fine exponent of the instrument in question*

# The Water Diviners

Treading the fields with his hazel twig
Showing farmers exactly where to dig
Parched crops wilting as far as eyes can see
Water hidden, over there, by the old yew tree
The water diviner struck liquid gold once again
A well sunk, the crops lifeblood soon to regain
Year after year, the farmer's gratitude enough
Brian the village legend always did his stuff

Is water divining passed on through generations?
There is one other, dowsing myriads of applications
Brian is his Uncle and yet his own path taken
Dowsing energy within the earth to awaken
Another time, another place, he explored his capability
His best-selling book on dowsing enhanced his credibility
Having read his words, Uncle Brian nodded sagely
This wise man's approval mattered to him greatly

Two men, both of the Earth, doing their divining thing
Hazel twig, rods or pendulum in their hands swing
Two generations united in a common purpose, a goal
Helping others selflessly, find water, go dig a hole

*Water diving or dowsing goes back far into the mists of time and to
many is still the best way to locate water in drought ridden country*

*areas. Check out my own best-selling book Unlock Your Life with Pendulum Dowsing if you would like to know more (shameless plug by your poet!)*

# Farming Through Time

He remembers his great grandfather
Wisdom etched in all the lines creasing his face
He said
"we don't own this land, we look after it for our sons and the
sons of our sons"
And this is how history unfolded
Down through countless generations
His own father before him
Grandad
Right back
The farm
Cared for
Nurtured
By those with the same surname
Passed down once again
Unbroken traditions
Five centuries of history
He feels it right there
In his blood
Walking this land of his ancestors
He feels it through the soles of his boots
Love for the soil
This place he cares for

Nurtured and farmed
Growing crops to feed the people
One day he will pass it on
He feels proud
The bloodline continues
The future assured
One day he knows
His daughter will take over

*An appreciation of those growers of the crops which feed us, farmers are not always given the respect they deserve and yet they provide for all of us*

# Island of My Mind

I would look from my window yonder
Untamed nature
Wild
Waves crashing upon beach
Heart of winter
Gales pounding
Residing here
Pioneering buccaneer
Safe in my sanctuary

Seasons change

I would share this transient place
My island
Wild
Waves lap gently upon beach
Heart of summer
Warming breeze
Growing here
Deeply see and hear
Safe in my paradise

*My dream to live on a smallish island, living by the seasons, acceptant of the extremes nature freely gives and feeling so creatively free in the process in return*

# Embracing Nature, Only Natural

PART ONE

Urban environment
Disassociated from nature
Only nature encountered
A green blur
Seen from car or train windows
Rushing on by
Us humans have a deep
You could call it primeval
Existing right there in our DNA
Connection to nature
Our nature to be found
Within nature
Zombie-like existence
Living a half life
All too disconnected from nature
Truly wild areas
Feared
Somewhere to be scared of
Living 24/7 in completely artificial environments
Killing creativity
Deadening intuition

Then comes the need
Real nature is encountered
Take some of this artificial Comfort Zone out there as well...

PART TWO

And I see them
Those walking deep within ancient tranquil forest
Climbing high upon a mountain
Canoeing upon tranquil river
Headphones on
Plugged into music
Maybe I miss out here?
My music collection stays at home
Rather than joining me on walks
In nature
Parallels drawn in my mind
Painted in words
A concert
Favourite band or symphony
Wearing a motorbike crash helmet
Ensuring only half the experience
Coming away disappointed
What was all the fuss about?
Sensory underload

PART THREE

To exercise in nature
First choice every time
Walking or running
Tai chi or meditating
Purest natural setting
Far from only taking exercise
Oh, such more than ever taking exercise
Inspirational
On every level
My best ideas
Poetry or life
How often one and the same
Those ground-breaking ideas
Popped into my head
As they usually do
Way out in the wilderness
Or in the middle of deserted ancient Neolithic site
And very rarely in the middle of a busy city...

*Large proportions of the populous have never been so disconnected
from nature, if I might be so bold as to make a suggestion? If you are
already appreciative of nature, and as you are reading this collection I
have the inkling you might be, please take your friends or family
members who haven't yet noticed the wonderful natural wonders
going on right now and allow them to see for themselves, let your
enthusiasm enthuse them*

# Today in this 21$^{st}$ Century

Today I pull up the drawbridge
My domain
My castle
None may enter

Today I go to the mountain
My niche
My cave
None may find me

Today I commune with nature
My forest
My seashore
None may follow

Today I bid adieu for a while
My freedom
My retreat
None may know

*The simpler life our ancestors knew...*

## Praise for Dean Fraser and his poetic work

These observational poems are thought provokingly deep, sometimes historical, other times contemporary and often simply laugh out loud funny...LANCASHIRE LIVING MAGAZINE

Dean Fraser sees his mission in life to spread some much needed laughter and love in this world INDIE SHAMAN MAGAZINE

It's lovely, life-affirming, amusing...SPIRITUAL ENGLAND

Be they inspirational or thought provoking...absorb yourself within these pages and leave the cares of the world behind for a little while. The author runs workshops helping people to live a more auspicious life PSYCHIC NEWS MAGAZINE

## Genuine reader book reviews

Nice content and pleased with it

Easy to read and informative

This is one book to have with you

## Audience members from his live shows

Listening to Dean Fraser transports you. Powerful works

Really enjoyed listening. I loved it, well done

Dean was very interactive with the audience afterwards and from that, he has offered to come back to do a session on how to meditate – a request from the audience

The originality of the poetry, easy listening

Listening to a very enjoyable poet, relaxing evening

Taking time out to relax and listening to an interesting and meaningful poet

A Guide to Making the Right Choices in Life

YOU

But Happier, Healthier and More Successful!

Dean Fraser

"Author shows how evolving comes from living, making mistakes which are not really mistakes but learning, walking our talk and sometimes tripping up a few times before we finally get the message about what we need in order to grow" NEW DAWN MAGAZINE.

**YOU But Happier** - Consciously making the choice to be a happier person is a real decision we can all make every single day. If being miserable can become habit-forming, Dean Fraser shows how to choose happiness instead.

**YOU But Healthier** - The best kind of changes which lead to a healthier way of being are those which can easily be integrated into our existing lifestyle. Taking small progressive steps to amazing holistic wellbeing are shown to be far simpler choices than ever imagined.

**YOU But More Successful** - Guidance taking the reader all the way to where they want to be within career and lifestyle. Rather than focussing solely on the financial factors, Dean Fraser encompasses all aspects of success and how living a more rewarding lifestyle needs to be an essential part of the journey to financial freedom.

## YOU But Happier, Healthier and More Successful by Dean Fraser
ISBN 9781548108830